2630344b

EUROPE

● WEISBADEN,
WEST GERMANY

AFRICA

AUSTRALIA

Author's Acknowledgments:

For special research for this book, I am deeply grateful to Joan Travis, Board of Directors, Institute of Human Origins, for giving me access to her personal files, and for inviting me into her home where Dr. Leakey and Biruté "hatched" the Orangutan Project; Antanas and Filomena Galdikas, Aldona Galdikas-Franz, and Maré Tiido, my guides through Biruté's childhood; the Camp Leakey staff, my guides through the Borneo rain forest; Gary Shapiro, Vice President, Orangutan Foundation International; Mary G. Smith, Senior Assistant Editor, National Geographic; the librarians at the Manhattan Beach Library; and Earthwatch.

My appreciation also to Liane B. Onish, Sid Iwanter, Byron Preiss, and Sue Cohen, for seeing potential in this writer; Gillian Bucky and Beverly Trainer, for meticulous editing; Chronicle Books; and my daughter Dawn, my proofreader and pillar of faith.

And finally, my loving gratitude to David Root, for believing in me, and for helping me fulfill my wildest dreams.

For my father, Carlos,
whose laughter lives on
in the hearts of his children.
—E. G.

Copyright © 1993 by Byron Preiss Visual Publications, Inc.
Text copyright © 1993 by Evelyn Gallardo
Afterword copyright © 1993 by Biruté Galdikas

The Great Naturalists™ is a trademark of
Byron Preiss Visual Publications, Inc.

Printed in Hong Kong

Front cover photograph copyright © by Evelyn Gallardo
Back cover photograph by Rod Brindamour, copyright © National Geographic Society

Photo Credits
Pages 6, 14, 27, 41, © Rod Brindamour; pages 8, 9 (top and middle), courtesy the Galdikas family;
page 9 (bottom), courtesy Maré Tiido; page 10 (top), © Joan Travis; page 10 (bottom), © Linda Flynn;
pages 11, 12, 13, 15, 16, 17, 18, 20, 22, 23, 29, 31, 32, © Evelyn Gallardo;
pages 24, 25, 26, 28, 30, 34, 36, 38, Rod Brindamour, © National Geographic Society;
pages 35, 37, © Gary Shapiro; page 39: Robert S. Oakes, © 1975 National Geographic Society.

Logo and jacket design by Stephen Brenninkmeyer
Map by John Pierard
Interior design concept by Cathleen O'Brien
Production by Nancy Novick, Rosana Ragusa, and Veronica Carmen

Special thanks to Victoria Rock, Jill Brubaker, and Kathy Huck
Library of Congress Cataloging-in-Publication Data

Gallardo, Evelyn.
   Among the orangutans : the Biruté Galdikas story / by Evelyn
Gallardo.
      p.   cm. — (The Great naturalists)
   " A Byron Preiss book."
   Includes index.
   Summary: Describes the life and research of Biruté Galdikas,
prominent expert on the behavior of orangutans in the wild.
   ISBN 0-8118-0031-8   ISBN 0-8118-0408-9 (pbk)
   1. Galdikas, Biruté Marija Filomina—Juvenile literature.
2. Women primatologists—Biography—Juvenile Literature.
3. Orangutan—Behavior—Research—Borneo—Juvenile literature.
4. Orangutan—Behavior—Research—Indonesia—Sumatra—Juvenile
literature. [1. Galdikas, Biruté Marija Filomena. 2. Zoologists.
3. Orangutan.]   I. Title   II. Series.
QL31.G34G35   1993
599.88' 42' 092—dc20
[B]   92-25777
                                                                   CIP
                                                                    AC

Distributed in Canada by Raincoast Books
8680 Cambie Street, Vancouver, B.C. V6P 6M9

10 9 8 7 6 5 4
Chronicle Books
85 Second Street
San Francisco, CA 94105

Web Site: www.chronbooks.com

AMONG THE ORANGUTANS
The Biruté Galdikas Story

◆

A Byron Preiss Book

◆

by Evelyn Gallardo

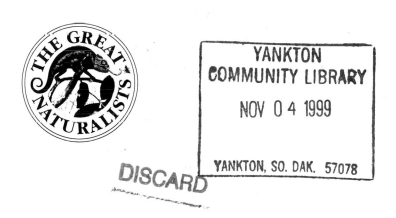

chronicle books·san francisco

TABLE OF CONTENTS

A Naturalist Is Born

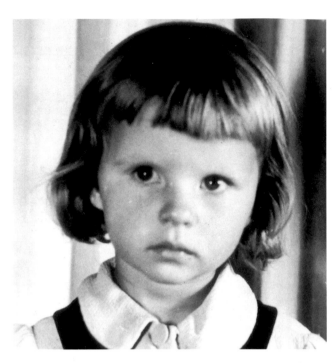

Biruté Galdikas was born in Weisbaden, West Germany, on May 10, 1946. Her parents had met at a refugee camp after fleeing their Lithuanian homeland at the end of World War II. Two years after she was born, Biruté's father signed a contract with the Canadian government to work its copper mines and the Galdikas family moved to Quebec. A year later, they settled in Toronto, Ontario.

Biruté's childhood was not unusual. She took ballet, piano, and violin lessons, and dreamed of being either a ballerina or an astronomer. Some of Biruté's dearest memories are of the times she spent with her best friend, Maré Tiido, and the Tiido family. The Tiidos had a cabin in the forest where they would spend their weekends fishing and exploring the woods. How Biruté looked forward to these trips! In fact, it was Maré's family who most inspired Biruté's love for the natural world.

As a little girl, Biruté loved to sit on her father's lap, picking out the countries on a spinning globe. She loved to gaze at the stars. And whenever she could, she would escape to the park near her house to climb trees and explore with her best friend Maré Tiido.

Biruté also had a special fondness for animals and enjoyed visiting the zoo, where she would spend hours watching the monkeys, apes, and lemurs. She was particularly fascinated by the great apes—chimpanzees, gorillas, and orangutans. Biruté learned that apes and humans are all mammals and members of the same family, and that the scientific name for this group is primates. Biruté also discovered that members of this group all share specific characteristics that link them together, such as hands that allow them to grasp things, the ability to stand upright, and a large, well-developed brain. More than any of the other primates, the behavior and facial expressions of the orangutans reminded Biruté of people. She longed to understand how they were related to humans and as she stared at the apes, she knew that one day she would learn more about them.

In 1962, the Galdikas family moved to Vancouver, in Western Canada. Soon her family moved again, this time to Southern California, where Biruté entered the University of California at Los Angeles to study psychology, archaeology, and anthropology.

All this time, Biruté's childhood fascination with orangutans continued. She still dreamed of finding a way to study these great apes. But because so little was known about orangutans and because their jungle habitat was so difficult to reach, no one seemed willing to fund a project to study them. So Biruté decided she would earn the money to pay for such a project herself. She was so focused on this dream that she had little time for anything else—certainly not boys or dating. But that soon changed.

One afternoon, while driving near the university, Biruté saw a young man standing on a corner. When he smiled at her, Biruté pulled the car over so quickly that she almost hit the curb. Only then did she notice that her brother was standing next to this handsome stranger. The stranger's name turned out to be Rod Brindamour, and within two years he and Biruté were married.

It was also during college that Biruté met another man who would change her life, Dr. Louis Leakey. Dr. Leakey was a paleontologist who was famous for having discovered thousands of fossils in Tanzania. One day, he came to the university to address Biruté's archaeology class. He talked about many things, including the importance of studying the behavior of humankind's closest living relatives, the great apes. Biruté was mesmerized. She felt certain that at last she had found the person who could help her realize her dream.

OPPOSITE: Biruté at age three.

TOP: Biruté's parents, Filomena and Antanas Galdikas.

MIDDLE: Eleven-year-old Biruté (right) with her father and younger siblings in Toronto.

BOTTOM: Biruté's childhood friend Maré Tiido with her parents in Ontario, Canada.

TOP: Biruté, Dr. Louis Leakey, and Rod discuss the Orangutan Project.

BOTTOM, left to right: Biruté, Jane Goodall, and Dian Fossey. Fossey was famous for her studies of mountain gorillas, Goodall for her work with chimpanzees.

After the lecture, Biruté boldly approached Dr. Leakey and asked him to help her launch a study of orangutans. Since he had helped fund other great ape projects, Biruté hoped he would do the same for her. Biruté was not the first person to make this request, however, and Dr. Leakey's response was less than encouraging. But when Biruté told him what she had already done to get the project underway, Dr. Leakey realized that Biruté was serious.

The next day a nervous Biruté met with the legendary Dr. Leakey. "I have not yet made up my mind about you," Dr. Leakey cautioned. "First, I want to give you a test."

"There are no hospitals in the rain forest, not even for emergency cases," he explained. "Are you willing to have your appendix removed?"

"Yes," Biruté replied eagerly, "and I will take my tonsils out, too, if you wish." Impressed by her commitment, Dr. Leakey selected Biruté to complete his primate-studying trio—Biruté, Jane Goodall, and Dian Fossey—the three women who would become known throughout the world as "Leakey's Primates." (Biruté never did have to have her appendix or tonsils removed because she soon figured out that Dr. Leakey was only testing her.)

Together, Dr. Leakey and Biruté began planning the Orangutan Project. The study would take place in Borneo, one of only two places where orangutans can be found in the wild. Dr. Leakey suggested that Biruté's husband accompany her to photograph the orangutans. After much discussion, Rod decided to put his computer science studies on hold to work with his wife.

In September 1971, three years after meeting Dr. Leakey, Biruté and Rod left Los Angeles bearing backpacks with only four changes of clothes between them and three *National Geographic* magazines. First, they stopped at the National

With Dr. Leakey's help, the Orangutan Project was eventually funded by the National Geographic Society and the Wilkie Brothers Foundation. Biruté prepared by going to the zoo as she had done as a child, this time studying the orangutans at the Los Angeles Zoo.

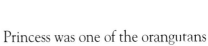

Princess was one of the orangutans that Biruté would meet in Borneo.

Geographic headquarters in Washington, D.C., for special photographic training and equipment. Then they flew to Kenya to visit Dr. Leakey, and afterward on to Tanzania for field training with Jane Goodall. Following stops in Pakistan, India, and Nepal, they flew to Indonesia.

Two to three million years ago, orangutans lived as far north as China and as far south as Java. As land bridges were formed by the shrinking seas of the Ice Age, orangutans traveled toward the equator in search of a warmer climate. Today, orangutans can only be found on the Indonesian islands of Borneo and Sumatra.

Biruté and Rod landed in Jakarta, the capital of Indonesia, two months after departing from Los Angeles. After meeting with forestry officials, Biruté learned that she would be based out of Tanjung Puting Reserve, a relatively unexplored area. When all the permits were in order, an official from the Forestry Department, Mr. Sugito, flew to Borneo with Rod and Biruté to introduce them to the local officials of Pangkalan Bun, the largest town near the study area.

From the window of the small airplane, Biruté stared at the rain forest below. The land was dense and green, except for the scattered clearings where people had burned the forest to grow rice, the mainstay of the Indonesian diet. Biruté was troubled by the vast clearings, for she knew that the orangutans, like many other

> Borneo was once colonized by both the Dutch and the British because of its wealth of natural resources such as spices, oil, natural gas, timber, gold, and diamonds. Today, it is a mixture of cultures that includes Chinese, Indian, Portuguese, Arabian, English, Dutch, and American.

OPPOSITE: Smoke from the burning rain forest hangs over the Sekonyer River.

RIGHT: The Pangkalan Bun marketplace, where Biruté and Rod bought their camp supplies.

Biruté at Camp Leakey.

creatures, depended on the rain forest to live. She realized that she would need to persuade the people to preserve the orangutans' vanishing rain forest habitat.

With Mr. Sugito to smooth the way, Biruté and Rod quickly completed their mandatory calls on local police, immigration, and forestry officials and were soon headed to the study area.

Accompanied by two forestry officials, Biruté and Rod loaded a small boat with supplies and set off up the Sekonyer River to their base camp thirty miles away. After many hours of paddling, they finally arrived. Biruté named their new home "Camp Leakey," in honor of her friend and mentor. Their new house was an abandoned loggers' hut, open on all four sides and built on stilts so that it stood high off the ground. While this would work temporarily, the couple soon realized they would need to build a more stable and permanent home. They decided to build their home out of ironwood, the only wood that would not rot in the humid rain forest. Six months later, they built another hut a mile and a half into the jungle, where they could cook meals and spend the night during long trackings. Biruté named the hut "Camp Wilkie," in honor of the brothers who had helped fund her research.

Biruté and Rod spent the first few days surveying the area around Camp Leakey. On their second day in camp, they spotted a female orangutan with an infant. The frightened orangutans took one look at Biruté and Rod and fled into the forest. For Biruté, that moment marked the beginning of a lifelong study of the shy and elusive Bornean orangutan.

Borneo and northern Sumatra are the last homes of Asia's only great ape. Sometimes called "red apes" because of their hair color, orangutans are one of the largest fruit-eaters on earth. They consume more than three hundred different fruits, bark, flowers, and occasionally eat insects and wild honey.

A mother and her infant make their way through the rain forest.

THE ORPHANS

In the Indonesian language, the meaning of *orang* is person, while *hutan* means forest. Orangutans, known as "Persons of the Forest," have inspired many myths. Some say that orangutans were once humans exiled to the trees for displeasing the gods. Another ancient Asian legend describes two birdlike creatures who were so tired from creating life on earth that they confused the formula for making humans. As the legend goes, they called their mistake "orangutan." Decades before, the native people of Borneo, called Dayaks, had been headhunters who believed human skulls held magic powers that could provide rain, increase the rice harvest, and prevent sickness. Today, Dayaks still whisper that orangutans are really ghosts who can vanish at will.

In reality, orangutans are shy mammals who have known humans only as enemies. Loggers destroy and exploit their rain forest home; poachers kill mother orangutans to sell their infants to zoos or as pets; and in the heart of Borneo, Dayaks still sometimes eat the apes. The charred bones of orangutans have been found with human fossils, which suggests that orangutans have been a source of human food dating as far back as thirty-five thousand years ago.

OPPOSITE: An orphan orangutan turns a rice sack into a hanging nest.

ABOVE: Mother orangutans exchange peeks at their new infants.

Because of their shy nature and impenetrable habitat, no one knows exactly how many orangutans there are in the wild, but estimates vary between five thousand and thirty thousand. Today, orangutans are endangered primarily because of poaching and loss of habitat.

17

A new arrival drinks powdered milk in the Camp Leakey nursery.

Although it is now illegal to own an orangutan, when Biruté arrived in Borneo many were kept as pets just outside the reserve area. Biruté was determined to return these apes to their natural habitat. She decided that if people knew that their pets could be taken away from them, perhaps they would think twice about buying them in the first place. As a result, the first Indonesian phrase that Rod learned was, "This officer is here with me so he can confiscate your orangutan." Embarrassed by the confrontation, most owners readily surrendered their pets.

Such was the case with the first young orangutan Biruté and Rod took from a man in Kumai, a town just outside the reserve. Biruté named the scrawny infant Sugito, in honor of the helpful forestry official. Sugito was about one year old, and his story was tragically familiar: his mother had been shot by a poacher who then sold the baby as a pet. Because the poachers have to shoot the mother orangutans in order to capture the babies, this means that every baby taken really equals the loss of two orangutans from the forest. It also means that there is one less female orangutan to produce new offspring.

While Biruté fed the orangutans she was trying to rehabilitate, she never fed the orangutans in the forest.

Biruté intended to release Sugito back into the wild, assuming that once he saw the rain forest, he would be anxious to return. This was hardly the case. Sugito insisted on staying near his rescuers, and since he was too young to go off on his own, Biruté, Rod, and their Indonesian assistant took turns carrying him as they walked through the forest. Each time he was given to a new "nanny," he would shriek in protest.

One morning, however, Biruté took the first shift and ended up carrying Sugito for the entire day. From that day forward, Biruté was his new mother. Sugito slept next to her at night, and clung to her while she ate and bathed. He made it almost impossible for Biruté to change clothes, and he attacked anyone who tried to take him from her. It was as though Sugito was permanently attached to Biruté's body.

Next followed Akmad, a shy six-year-old who had been taken from a loggers' camp. Not long after Akmad was rescued, another confiscated baby orangutan came to live at Camp Leakey. Biruté named the newcomer Sobiarso, in honor of a helpful police official. Sugito was not at all happy with these newcomers and fiercely defended his number–one position with Biruté.

Each new arrival was quarantined for two weeks to prevent it from spreading disease to the other fragile orphans. The orangutans were fed rice, fruit, and powdered milk.

When the milk wasn't mixed to their liking, they sprayed it onto the walls of the hut. In fact, nothing was safe from the curious apes. They unmercifully shredded clothing to make nests, drank shampoo, ate toothpaste, took apart flashlights, and even tore open the couple's mattress to eat the seeds in the stuffing. To the young orangutans, everything was a toy.

But despite all the excitement the orphaned orangutans brought to the camp, the first two months of research were frustrating. Biruté woke up each morning long before daylight to search for wild orangutans, and she returned at dusk each night drenched by rain, caked with mud, and bleeding from leech bites.

Biruté quickly learned to walk quietly through the forest and to listen for clues. The sound of fruit pits or bark hitting the ground was a telltale sign that an orangutan was eating nearby. More than once, she heard crashing branches as an orangutan traveled through the trees, only to lose the animal in the dense rain forest. On a few occasions, Biruté tracked slower-moving females with infants for up to two or three hours, but as soon as the apes realized they were being followed, they threw broken branches at her and loudly smacked their lips and grunted in protest. But she knew that only through repeated contact would she be able to earn the orangutans' trust. With this in mind, she endured their assaults with as much humor and grace as possible. Biruté once searched for ten days before spotting an ape, but she had heard of a Japanese scientist who had searched for two months without seeing a single orangutan. At least she was finding them.

Unlike the highly social chimpanzees, gorillas, and bonobos who travel in groups on the ground, orangutans live alone in the trees and travel by swinging through the dense treetops. Biruté soon discovered that the most difficult thing about studying orangutans was finding them.

OPPOSITE: Orangutans travel by swinging from tree to tree, which makes it difficult to find them.

DISCOVERIES

One day, Biruté came upon a female with a small infant clinging to her side and an older offspring on her back. The mother moved slowly through the trees, fleeing from what was most likely the first human she had ever seen. Biruté would have no trouble remembering this trio, and she named them Fran, Fern, and Freddy, after some of Rod's family and friends.

Biruté only named an orangutan when she was sure to recognize it the next time it appeared, and she followed Jane Goodall's example of keeping track of related apes by beginning their names with the same letter of the alphabet. Biruté named one male Throat Pouch, or "T. P.," because of the large throat pouch under his chin. Biruté used size as well as the color, pattern, and amount of hair on the animals' backs, or an unusual trait such as a stiff or missing finger, to tell one orangutan from another. With time, she discovered that individual orangutans are as unique as individual humans.

Adult female orangutans weigh between seventy and eighty pounds, while adult males can weigh over two hundred pounds. Biruté differentiated between males and females by their size, but also by identifying the males' distinctive throat pouch and cheek pads.

Biruté's first real breakthrough came two months after their arrival when she and Rod spotted a female orangutan with a two-year-old infant. Following them for the entire day, they saw that the mother moved slowly, doing little but eat and gaze into the distance. Biruté and Rod kept up with her until she nested high in a tree for the night. This

OPPOSITE: A female orangutan with her offspring.

RIGHT: A male orangutan exhibits the characteristic cheek pads.

ABOVE: A mother orangutan keeps her infant close to her as she wades through a swamp.

OPPOSITE: An infant practices building a nest out of leaves and branches.

was very important, for now Biruté knew where to find her the next morning. She named the pair Beth and Bert.

Biruté followed Beth and Bert for five days without seeing another orangutan. She observed that Beth and other orangutan mothers never let their young out of their sight. Infants did not begin to explore away from their mothers' bodies until they were about one year old. Even then, they usually stayed within arm's reach. Biruté's early observations seemed to confirm the reports of other scientists: Except for the relationship between a mother and her offspring, orangutans spend most of their time alone. Still, Biruté couldn't help wondering if this was really true.

Another mother, whom Biruté called Cara, was pregnant and beginning to encourage the independence of her eight-year-old son, Carl. More than once, Biruté saw Cara chase and bite Carl. When he tried to share Cara's nest, she pushed him away, while he shrieked in protest. After several unsuccessful attempts to get back into his mother's nest, Carl reluctantly moved to another tree and made a nest of his own. At other times, perhaps to soften the blow of separation, Cara playfully swatted at Carl. This proved to Biruté that the bond between mother orangutans and their offspring is very strong.

Later, Cara provided Biruté with one of her most exciting glimpses into orangutan sociability. One day, Biruté watched Cara and Carl meet another mother and son, whom Biruté named Priscilla and Pug. Soon, Beth, Bert, and an adolescent male orangutan Biruté had never seen before, joined them. This was the first time Biruté had ever seen so many orangutans together.

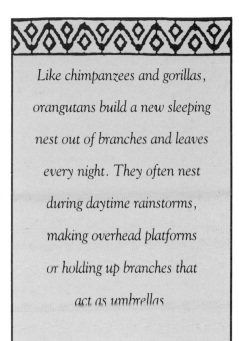

Like chimpanzees and gorillas, orangutans build a new sleeping nest out of branches and leaves every night. They often nest during daytime rainstorms, making overhead platforms or holding up branches that act as umbrellas

Another day when Biruté was hiking through the jungle, she swung her machete through a vine and accidentally gashed her knee. Because the injury was too serious to tend to in the field, Biruté was forced to head back to Camp Leakey. To save time and avoid the leeches, she took a shortcut. Limping through an overgrown rice field, Biruté intently watched the ground for snakes and holes. When she looked up again, she gasped. A huge male orangutan was walking through the tall grass ahead of her. Incredibly, he was about four hundred and fifty feet from the forest. Biruté was the first person in the world to see a wild orangutan so far from the forest. She had made another important discovery: that male orangutans will venture out from the safety of the forest.

Biruté's next breakthrough came while she and Rod sat watching T. P. eat in a tree above them. Suddenly, T. P. charged down

the tree, looked at Biruté and Rod for several seconds, and then dropped to the ground and began to claw for termites. From then on, Biruté saw T. P. come down to the ground almost daily, an indication that orangutans will search for food on the ground as well as in trees. On another occasion, Biruté stumbled upon a lone male orangutan sleeping on the ground. Before this discovery, orangutans had been known to nest only in trees. Biruté was the first scientist to see a wild orangutan asleep on the ground.

On another day, Biruté saw T. P. chase off a male who had been pursuing Priscilla. T. P. then followed Priscilla from tree to tree while she foraged for fruit. Suddenly, a large adult male orangutan Biruté had never seen before appeared ahead of them. He, too, must have sensed that Priscilla was ready to mate, and the two males began a violent battle. They bit, pounded, chased, and wrestled, falling from the trees several times. Then, abruptly, they stopped fighting and stared at one another. Soon the furious battle resumed, until twenty minutes later, they moved to opposite trees and stared at each other again. T. P. let out a spine-tingling roar and snapped a dead tree in half. As the tree toppled, T. P.'s larger opponent dropped to the ground and vanished. Biruté was the first scientist to witness combat between two male orangutans in the wild.

Finally Biruté was beginning to feel that her research was getting somewhere. On most days, the apes did little more than eat, rest, and travel, and others with less determination than Biruté might have given up long before they had had a chance to observe such events. But Biruté was patient and persistent, and because of this she had learned information about orangutans that no other scientist had been able to discover.

Although Biruté's research continued to reveal new and interesting data, by the end of the first year, the jungle had taken its toll on the young couple. Existing mainly on a diet of rice and canned sardines, with some occasional fresh fish, Biruté and Rod had each lost more than twenty pounds. The humidity had rotted their boots, their clothes were tattered, and they suffered from mysterious infections, boils, and sores. In addition, a doctor had overprescribed their anti-malaria pills. As a result, Biruté and Rod began to suffer from blurred and double vision.

Then, during the last week in September 1972, Biruté had several dreams about death, but she woke up each morning unable to remember the details. On October 1st, she turned on the radio. The reception was terrible—mostly just crackling sounds—but suddenly the words became clear. Dr. Louis Leakey had died of a massive heart attack. After a year in the jungle, Biruté had lost her friend and mentor. Now, she, too, felt like an orphan of the forest.

Biruté records her discoveries.

QUEEN OF THE ORANGUTANS

It took weeks for Biruté to recover from the devastating shock of Dr. Leakey's death. Biruté doubted her ability to carry on without his support. Now she had to do more than simply record information and stick to her detective work; she would also have to be a writer and a fundraiser. She had no idea that prior to his death, Dr. Leakey had made it known that the Orangutan Project was his number-one priority. He had left a legacy of friends, like Jane Goodall, who offered to help Biruté and convinced others to do the same. She was determined to be worthy of their trust.

Even as death haunted Biruté's thoughts, new life sprang forth in the form of a tiny infant born to Cara. Biruté named the newborn Cindy, and she followed Cara, Cindy, and Carl for thirty-one days. During this time, Cara stopped throwing branches at Biruté. It seemed she had finally accepted the primatologist's presence.

Biruté watched the orangutans mate and produce healthy offspring and was encouraged by the thought that slowly, the orangutan population was naturally growing, ensuring their continued existence. Biruté was beginning to unravel the mysteries surrounding orangutan social life. Fern no longer traveled with her mother, Fran, but

Before Biruté's revealing study, the only information about orangutan births had come from zoos. When confined to captivity, female orangutans give birth every three or four years. But after observing Beth, Fran, and several other mothers, Biruté determined that wild orangutans have offspring only about every eight or nine years.

OPPOSITE: It took months for the orangutans to learn to trust Biruté.

RIGHT: The orphans were fed a twice-daily meal of milk, rice, and fruit.

instead had started traveling, playing, and grooming with two other adolescents named Maud and Georgina. This friendship lasted until Georgina had a baby. When Fern and Maud later gave birth to their own infants, Georgina once again resumed her interest in her old friends. Their relationship had changed, however. Mother orangutans raise their young by them-selves, so with an offspring comes the added responsibility of finding enough food for two. The new mothers can no longer afford to spend as much time with their friends.

Eight and a half months after mating with T. P., Priscilla gave birth to a baby Biruté called Pete. After the birth, T. P. suddenly disappeared, and though Biruté listened for his distinctive call and searched for him for several days, he was nowhere to be found. The only explanation she could think of was that he had died. Biruté felt like she had lost an old friend.

More than two years later, T. P. mysteriously returned. Biruté was baffled: where had he gone, and why had he come back? Biruté concluded that either adult male orangutans were nomadic wanderers or they used much larger home ranges than previously imagined. Because Biruté had consistently encountered females within specific ranges, she concluded that females maintained stable areas and that these ranges were much smaller than those of the males.

During these observations, Biruté began to notice some patterns. Adult females mingled with both males and females of all age groups, while adolescents mingled with each other

The orangutan long call is used to keep other males away, while hopefully drawing females toward them. During a long call, the caller shakes branches or topples dead trees while sending out a fearsome roar that can last several minutes. The call can be heard nearly a mile away, and the first time Biruté heard one, she thought it was the most frightening sound in the forest.

and with adult females. Adult males, however, proved to be much less sociable than females or adolescent orangutans. While they accepted females of all ages, adult male orangutans avoided other males, except to fight one another in the presence of a female ready to mate. This is quite different from other great apes.

Biruté discovered that orangutans also communicate quite differently from other apes. Unlike the group-living apes who communicate with their own "languages" of sounds, facial expressions, postures, and behavior, orangutans spend a great deal of time alone and appear to have had little reason to develop complex forms of communication. The most basic form of orangutan communication is the "long call," which is used only by mature males.

As Biruté watched and listened to the orangutans in the forest, she noticed that Carl was continually scratching his skin. Then Cara and Cindy began to show the same

OPPOSITE: Nick.

RIGHT: Orangutans like to eat bark and pulp from trees.

An orangutan sits on the remains of an observation tower once used to spot orangutans in the forest.

symptoms. Biruté watched in horror as their conditions grew worse, and one day she saw Cara carrying Cindy's limp body. For days, Cara groomed Cindy, sometimes holding her to her breast as though encouraging her to suckle. Finally, Cara cradled Cindy one last time and then left her dead body in the nest. Although Biruté sent organ and skin samples from Cindy's body to laboratories for testing, no one was able to determine why Cindy had died.

In the next few months, Carl and then Cara disappeared from the forest. Biruté knew the possibility of finding their bodies was slim, and the loss was almost too much for her to bear. She had not prepared for the deaths of these friends. It was not until years later, when Biruté was analyzing her data, that she realized a prolonged rainy season had kept many trees from bearing fruit, forcing the orangutans to eat unusually large amounts of bark. Malnutrition was the most likely cause of their deaths.

While Biruté mourned the death of her friends, National Geographic came to Borneo to film Biruté's life with the orangutans. In October 1975, they published an article she wrote, complete with photographs taken by Rod. Later, an Italian magazine wrote an article about Biruté that was appropriately titled "Queen of the Orangutans," for Biruté now knew more about these apes than anyone else on earth.

By this time four years had passed, and more than twenty orphans in various phases of being reintroduced into the wild were in and around Camp Leakey. Most of the orphans were slowly venturing farther and farther into the forest, but Sugito was another story altogether. Although he had been ferried to a feeding station across the river with nine of the oldest orphans, Sugito always managed to return to Biruté. Biruté began to worry that her first orphan might never adjust to the wild. Soon her worries became very real.

One day that summer, the youngest orphan was found drowned in the river. Several weeks later, Biruté and Rod arrived just in time to rescue another baby that Sugito was holding facedown in the water. And a few months later, one of Biruté's favorite orphans, called Doe, was found drowned by the river. The other orphans quickly gathered together, confused by Doe's motionless body. But not Sugito. Instead he approached the corpse, waving his arms in front of him. When Biruté looked into his eyes, she knew that Sugito had killed Doe and the other orphan. Because wild orangutans are not known to kill each other, Biruté believed that Sugito murdered out of jealousy. Biruté could not bring herself to banish Sugito from the camp, but she knew that from that day forward they would have to watch him very carefully.

From observing wild orangutans, Biruté learned that the best way to wean the orphans was to physically distance herself from them as they grew older. In order to encourage the orphans to wander farther into their natural habitat, two feeding stations were built—one just across the river and another about eight hundred feet into the forest.

During her time in the rain forest, Biruté had lost touch with the world outside Camp Leakey. She had begun to think of the orphans as her unruly children, but all this changed when she gave birth to her first child on October 17, 1976. They named him Binti Paul Galdikas Brindamour. In one Indonesian dialect, a *binti* is a small bird. It was also the name of an official who had helped Biruté and Rod when they first arrived in Borneo.

After five years of devoting herself to the world of orangutans, Binti brought

Biruté back in touch with the human world. After playing mother to orangutan orphans, she now had her own son to nurture and love. But raising a child in the jungle had its problems. Before Binti was a year old, he began imitating an orphan named Princess. Binti followed Princess everywhere. Together they scurried like siblings exploring the world around them, often getting into mischief.

Meanwhile, although Sugito had stopped killing orphan orangutans, his behavior was still a problem. He bit the assistants and the cooks, and it seemed that his bad habits were starting to rub off on some of the other orphans. Although Biruté felt sure Sugito would never harm Binti, the boy was constantly watched.

Some days when Biruté went into the forest, she took Binti with her. When he pointed at monkeys, trees, flying squirrels, flying snakes, or flying lizards, she taught him both their Indonesian and English names. Binti even scanned the treetops to help her find orangutans.

OPPOSITE: Binti and Princess were inseparable playmates.

By 1978, seven years after their arrival, Biruté had logged twelve thousand hours of orangutan observation and Camp Leakey had grown from a single loggers' hut to eight permanent buildings.

The staff had also grown. One of the new staff members was a native Dayak named Pak Bohap, who had been hired as a tree-climber to locate wild orangutans. Biruté learned that Bohap's grandfather had been one of seven Dayak rulers. Another staff member was Gary Shapiro, a graduate student from the University of Oklahoma. Gary had come to Camp Leakey to teach American Sign Language to Sugito because Biruté hoped to learn directly from Sugito why he had killed Doe and the others. Sugito, however, refused to cooperate, so Gary began to work with some of the other orphans. He would cup an orangutan's hand in his own, carefully moving it to form various signs. Naturally, the first signs the orangutans learned were food oriented. When they signed correctly, Gary would reward them with cookies or other treats. To two-year-old Binti, Gary was known as "Mr. Cookie."

Although Gary never taught Binti sign language, the boy quickly picked it up. Soon he began signing to all the orangutans, whether they were Gary's pupils or not. Biruté and Rod continued to worry about their son, for he had not grown out of the habit of imitating orangutans. They were concerned

Biruté hoped that by teaching sign language to orangutans in their native habitat she could learn what was important to them.

that without human playmates, Binti would have social problems when he grew older.

At the same time, Sugito's raids on the camp started getting worse. One day, while Biruté was away, Sugito broke into the house and ransacked the medicine cabinet, smashing bottles and throwing pills everywhere. When Rod discovered the mess, he decided that it was time to let Sugito go free. He took Sugito many miles from camp and released him into the forest. When Biruté returned, she sadly accepted the news. Sugito was never seen again.

The following year, Rod began to grow restless. He had never expected they would stay in the rain forest more than a few years, but Rod could see that Biruté's life in Borneo was permanent. Biruté could not change Rod's mind, and regretfully they decided to separate. Rod left for Canada to pursue a career in computer science. He soon announced plans to remarry, which led Biruté to make the most difficult decision of her life.

Binti's orangutan imitations were still a serious concern. Although Biruté hated to admit it, she realized that Binti needed contact with other children. She knew that Jane Goodall had sent her son to London after experiencing a similar situation. For Binti's sake, Biruté tearfully took him to live with Rod and his new wife.

OPPOSITE: Gary signs to Rinnie as Biruté and two other orangutans look on.

BELOW: Biruté and Binti hike through the rain forest.

THE FUTURE

After more than a decade of living with orangutans in their rain forest habitat and carefully analyzing her data, Biruté had finally begun to piece together central parts of the orangutan puzzle. She had learned that the early portraits of the orangutan as a social recluse were wrong. Because of their reclusive nature, orangutans appeared at first to be solitary animals. But Biruté had learned that they do have contact with each other, only much more rarely and in a more limited way than other primates. Biruté concluded that only by keeping to themselves could these large animals survive. If they lived in groups, they would have to travel much farther to find enough food.

Biruté's life in Borneo has changed drastically since her arrival in 1971. After Rod and Binti left Borneo, Pak Bohap began to play an increasingly important role. His botanical skills and his ability to locate wild orangutans proved invaluable. He heard sounds in the forest that no one else could hear, and he detected movements which Biruté might otherwise have missed. Equally important, he taught Biruté more about Indonesian culture. His companionship gave her the strength to continue with the Orangutan Project, and in 1981, they were married. They now have two children, a daughter, Jane, named for Biruté's good friend and colleague Jane Goodall, and a son named Frederick.

There have been changes in the orangutans' world as well, some of which are very discouraging. Many of the trusted forestry officials who helped Biruté in the early years have been replaced by others who are more interested in money than orangutans. Today, several hundred baby orangutans are smuggled out of Borneo under false export permits each year.

In 1974, Indonesia issued a silver coin to help raise money to save the endangered orangutan. This coin has a face value of five thousand rupiahs (or two dollars) and features the animal it was created to save.

OPPOSITE: Biruté and an orphan travel by canoe on the Sekonyer River.

In 1984, several people from Earthwatch, an organization that sends volunteers to do fieldwork with scientists, saw an orangutan eat two squirrels. This was an exciting discovery because no one had ever seen a wild orangutan eat meat. The discovery clearly showed that there was still much more to be learned about these fascinating animals.

Because few of the infants reach their destinations alive, smugglers ship several babies for each one they intend to sell. They are sent to places like Singapore, Thailand, and Taiwan, where they are sold in open markets.

In 1990, officials at the Bangkok airport in Thailand X-rayed two suspicious-looking crates, labeled "LIVE BIRDS." Each crate contained three baby orangutans who had been drugged and packed in tight compartments without food or water. Three of them had been shipped upside-down, and several had pneumonia. With Biruté's help, the "Bangkok Six" were eventually nursed back to health and flown back home to Borneo. But other captured orangutans haven't been so lucky.

Orangutans face many other problems as well. Loggers are destroying their habitat at an uncontrollable rate, cutting roads deep into the forest that make it easy for poachers to find the orangutans. Many Indonesians are moving to Borneo from Java and other islands, and in order to grow enough food to feed them all, they use a method of planting fields called slash-and-burn, which ruins the rain forest.

However, there are also promising developments which indicate that Indonesia is slowly changing its ways. The setting aside of nature preserves such as Tanjung Puting and Gunung Leuser in nothern Sumatra as well as strict laws to protect the forests in Indonesia and Malaysia are all encouraging signs that orangutans will have a better chance for survival in their native habitat in the future.

With the help of friends, Biruté has formed a non-profit organization called the Orangutan Foundation. Its purpose is to prevent the extinction of orangutans and their rain forest habitat by raising money to fund research, conservation, and educational programs.

Biruté quickly became a surrogate parent to many young orangutans.

In 1991, Biruté celebrated twenty years of studying orangutans. In the process, she has become the world's authority on these mysterious apes. Yet, she hasn't found all the answers. How long do they live? How far do they range? How many offspring do they have? These questions could take a lifetime to answer, and Biruté has decided to devote her life to doing just that.

AFTERWORD

For over twenty years, I have been studying orangutans in the remote tropical rain forests of Borneo. When I began my work in 1971, very little was known about wild orangutans. The challenge ahead of me was an exciting one.

I started the Orangutan Project in Borneo with only the help of my husband, Rod Brindamour. Now I have many people from all over the world working with me. My hope is to collect enough data on orangutan life so that we can better understand the forces that shape their lives in the wild. I hope to observe orangutans for the rest of my life and that my Indonesian students will continue the study long after I am gone.

Evelyn Gallardo and I have been friends for many years. She has visited me twice in Borneo and has also spent time in Rwanda with mountain gorillas. She is one of the few people in the world who has observed and photographed both wild orangutans and gorillas in their native habitat. Upon her return from Borneo and Africa, Evelyn developed a great-ape education program for school children in Southern California. Her life is now dedicated to helping wild orangutans and mountain gorillas survive.

Although this book is the story of my life, Evelyn lived through a part of it, too. She has observed firsthand many of the situations she describes in this text. I thank Evelyn for creating this book so that children all over the world can share my experiences. I hope her words and pictures will inspire generations of naturalists to carry on the work of the scientists that have come before them. I have tremendous faith in children because they are eager and willing to improve our environment. We share this fragile home planet with many other creatures, and it is up to all of us to respect and protect them.

Biruté Galdikas

Organizations

Orangutan Foundation International
822 South Wellesley Avenue
Los Angeles, CA 90049
(310) 207-1655

Other Organizations:

Earthwatch
680 Mount Auburn Street
P.O. Box 403N
Watertown, MA 02272-9104
(617) 926-8200

International Primate Protection League
P.O. Box 766
Summerville, SC 29484
(803) 871-2280

The L. S. B. Leakey Foundation
77 Jack London Square, Suite M
Oakland, CA 94607-3750
(510) 834-3636

National Geographic Society
17th and M Street, N.W.
Washington, DC 20036
(202) 857-7000

Rainforest Action Network
450 Sansome, Suite 700
San Francisco, CA 94111
(415) 398-4404

GLOSSARY

Anthropology: The study of humans.

Archaeology: The study of artifacts and other material remains of past human life.

Bonobo: The fourth great ape, found only in Zaire and recognized as a separate species in 1929.

Data: Information gathered about a particular subject.

Dayaks: The native people of Borneo.

Endangered species: A species that is in serious danger of becoming extinct.

Extinct: No longer in existence.

Fieldwork: The gathering of information about an animal by observing it in its natural habitat.

Fossil: A preserved rock or impression of an animal or plant from prehistoric times.

Great apes: A group of apes consisting of chimpanzees, gorillas, orangutans, and bonobos.

Habitat: A place where groups of plants and animals naturally live and grow.

Home range: The area to which the activities of an animal or group of animals are confined.

Long call: A vocal sound made by male orangutans to warn other males to stay away from their territory and to attract females.

Malaria: A human disease caused by the bite of an infected tropical mosquito.

Mammal: Any warm-blooded animal, including primates, usually having hair covering its skin. Mothers give birth to live young and feed them with milk from mammary glands.

Mate: A male or female member of a breeding pair of animals.

Naturalist: A person who studies plants, animals, or environments.

Nature preserve: An area of land that is protected from human activity and allowed to remain in its natural state.

Natural resources: Materials used by humans that are supplied by nature, i.e., oil, iron, coal, water.

Offspring: The natural young of an animal.

Paleontology: The study of fossils and extinct forms of life.

Poacher: A person who kills or sells animals illegally.

Primates: A group of mammals that consists of humans, apes, monkeys, lemurs, and tarsiers.

Primatology: The study of primates other than humans.

Quarantine: To isolate for a period of time in order to prevent the spread of disease.

Rain forest: Dense, tropical forest that receives heavy rainfall.

Rehabilitate: To restore or bring to a healthy condition.

Sign language: The use of hands instead of words as a form of communication.

Sociability: The degree to which an animal associates with others of the same species.

Species: A group of animals or plants that breed with one another and share similar physical characteristics.

Territory: An area that is occupied and defended by an animal or group of animals.

Throat pouch: Extra skin attached to the throat of an adult male orangutan that varies in size and shape. It helps increase the sound of the long call. (Some females also grow small throat pouches.)

EUROPE

• WEISBADEN,
WEST GERMANY

AFRICA

AUSTRALIA